Chicken Boots

NEWMAN SPRINGS PUBLISHING
320 Broad Street
Red Bank, NJ 07701

First originally published by Newman Springs Publishing 2024

ISBN 979-8-89061-364-6 (Paperback)
ISBN 979-8-89061-365-3 (Digital)

Printed in the United States of America

Chicken Boots

Olivia Reuter

My name is Kayla. I am four. I want to go to a big-screen movie. My mommy and daddy go to some. I tried to go to one, but there was a scary part—a super scary part. I didn't like that at all!

My mommy took me to a movie last month at the theater in our town. I was so excited! We drove by the theater a lot in our car, but I'd never been in it. I asked my mommy and daddy over and over what it was like inside that big building. I felt so much bigger and older today; this was my first time at a movie ever! My two-year-old sister didn't get to go; she had to stay home with Daddy. It was just Mommy and me, and I was so excited!

First, we walked into the big door with a big poster of a pretty princess on a horse. I wondered if we would see that movie—I hoped so! We waited in a line, then Mommy paid the person at the counter. She said, "One adult and one child," and handed the man some money. He gave her some papers. Mommy said, "Kayla, these are our tickets."

Then, we walked down the hall. I smelled popcorn; it smelled so good. Then I saw a counter with lots of candy in the glass! I'd never seen so much candy before! Wow! I hoped my mommy would buy me some, but she got me something better! She ordered me a kids' special snack tray. The tray had princesses and robots and animals on it. It had spaces for popcorn and a fruit snack and a soda pop. I picked the orange kind of soda pop. It was so bubbly and yummy! I'd never had it before!

PoP Corn
Coca Cola

After I had my tray and Mommy had her popcorn, we went into the theater to pick our seats. My mommy got me a cover to put on my seat so it wouldn't flip up while I was sitting on it. I was a little scared—the theater was this big, huge room, and it was kind of dark, and there were all these people. But I saw other kids with their mommies or their daddies, so it was okay. I sat down by my mommy and started eating my popcorn. It was so buttery; it was the best popcorn I ever had! There was a place to put my cup in my seat like in my car seat.

All of a sudden, loud music started playing. It was super loud, and then the theater got darker and darker. I was scared. I grabbed on to my mommy and hugged her tight. Then, they started showing parts of other movies. I was confused. Mommy told me they called those previews and the movie we came to see would be on next. I got used to the loud noise and sat in my own chair, just holding my mommy's hand.

There was more loud music, and then there were cartoon people playing and talking. I didn't know what they were doing, but it was so nice to have a TV so big to watch a show on! There were bright colors, and the people were so happy. But then everything turned dark, and they showed this scary guy with scary yellow eyes and big teeth! It was a monster! I grabbed on to my mommy again and shut my eyes. The scary guy kept talking; I was so scared. My mommy said, "Kayla, you are okay. Just shut your eyes. Mommy is right here."

I was almost crying. I said, "Mommy, we need to leave. I don't like it!" I heard other kids crying, too, and some others leaving. My mommy said, "Kayla, it's okay, we can try another movie another time. I didn't know this scary part was in the movie. I'm sorry, honey."

My mommy carried me out of the theater. We brought my snack tray too. When I was out of there, I stopped crying. It was good to see light again! We walked outside; it was sunny and warm. I felt so much better!

My mommy helped me get in my car seat, and we started driving home. I was tired. I imagined making my own movie. If I was a moviemaker person, I'd make a funny movie with no scary parts. I would have a chicken in my movie. The chicken would have yellow boots and would be dancing. The chicken would walk around the playground with kids and sing. They would go down the slide and swing into the sky. It would be a happy and fun movie. No one scary would ever come on the screen. Kids would like to come to the movies, and no one would cry or be scared. More kids could go to the movies, and it would be awesome!

Suddenly, I heard my mommy say, "Kayla, wake up. We are home." I think I fell asleep. I didn't remember the ride at all, just the chicken in boots. I really wanted to see this chicken! Maybe someday I will make my own movie!